DO GOLDFISH FLY?

No! Hummingbirds fly.

Hummingbirds are very small birds that can fly very quickly! Their wings flap so fast they make a humming sound. Hummingbirds can fly up, down, left and right. They can fly forwards, backwards and even upside down!

DO GOLDFISH HOP?

No! Kangaroos hop.

Kangaroos use their huge hind legs to hop from place to place. They can hop much faster than people can run. Their long tails swing up and down to help them hop.

DO GOLDFISH PADDLE?

No! Ducks paddle.

A duck has wide, webbed feet. Webbed feet have flaps of skin between the toes. They help the duck paddle through water.

DO GOLDFISH POUNCE?

No! Pumas pounce.

A puma pounces on other animals from behind. It has thick pads on the bottoms of its paws. The pads help the cat move silently and surprise its prey. The puma's powerful legs spring into action for long leaps.

DO GOLDFISH SLITHER?

No! Snakes slither.

A snake slithers in a smooth and slinky wave.
It glides over grass and twists around tree
trunks. Strong muscles help its long, scaly
body move smoothly over the ground.

DO GOLDFISH CLIMB?

No! Geckos climb.

Gecko lizards can climb straight up a slippery
window. They scoot up and down trees and
walls. They scale smooth rocks. Special pads on
a gecko's toes help the lizard climb and cling.

DO GOLDFISH SWING THROUGH TREES?

No! Gibbons swing through trees.

Gibbons have long arms that help them swing from branch to branch. Tall trees are safe places for gibbons to sleep, eat and play.

DO GOLDFISH DIG THROUGH DIRT?

No! Earthworms dig through dirt.

Earthworms dig in the dark, damp dirt. They push forward with open mouths. As they move they swallow dirt and bits of dead plants. Earthworms leave the dirt looser and richer.

DO GOLDFISH JUMP THROUGH GRASS?

No! Grasshoppers jump through grass.

thighs

Grasshoppers have thick, powerful thighs.
Their legs bend backward. Grasshoppers' special
legs help them jump through the tallest grass.
Grasshoppers can jump up to 20 times their own
body length!

DO GOLDFISH CRAWL?

No! **Spiders crawl.**

Spiders crawl around using eight long legs.
They can crawl almost anywhere, even on ceilings!
Spiders have claws and tiny hairs on the ends of
their legs. The hairs help them stick to things.

DO GOLDFISH GALLOP?

No! Zebras gallop.

Zebras run swiftly! They can gallop like horses. Most zebras live on open grasslands. They have few places to hide. Some animals try to attack them. They must run quickly to get away.

DO GOLDFISH SWIM?

Yes! Goldfish swim.

Shimmering goldfish are
sleek and slim.
Shimmering goldfish
swish and swim!

How and where animals move

Animals move above our heads.

swing and sway → gibbons
climb and cling → geckos
flap and hum → hummingbirds

a gibbon hanging from a fruit tree

Animals move below our feet.

slither and slink → snakes
dig and wiggle → earthworms
creep and crawl → spiders

a slithery snake

a mandarin duck

Animals move through the water.

paddle and splash → ducks

swish and swim → goldfish

Animals hop and jump and race.

pad and pounce → pumas

hop around → kangaroos

jump really high → grasshoppers

Animals run with other animals.

gallop in large groups → zebras

zebras galloping in the water

GLOSSARY

gallop run so fast that all four legs leave the ground at once

muscle one of the parts of the body that help you move, lift or push

pounce leap on something and grab it

prey animal that is hunted by another animal for food

scale climb up or over

silent completely quiet or without noise

slither slide along. Snakes have no legs, so they have to slither instead of walk.

thighs upper part of some animals' legs. A grasshopper's strong thighs help it jump far.

webbed feet feet that have flaps of skin between the toes. Webbed feet help ducks paddle.

COMPREHENSION QUESTIONS

1. Which animals swing through trees?
2. Snakes slither through the grass. What does "slither" mean?
3. Ducks and goldfish are animals that move through the water. What other animals swim in the water?

READ MORE

Flying Frogs and Walking Fish, Robin Page and Steve Jenkins (Houghton Mifflin Harcourt, 2016)

Giraffes Can't Dance, Giles Andreae (Orchard Books, 2014)

Learning About Animals (The Natural World), Catherine Veitch (Raintree, 2014)

WEBSITES

www.bbc.co.uk/education/clips/zpwkjxs
This video clip explores how animals move.

www.oum.ox.ac.uk/thezone/animals/life/move.htm
This website shows how an animal's skeleton helps
it move.

www.sciencekids.co.nz/animals.html
Learn amazing facts about animals.

LOOK FOR ALL THE BOOKS IN THE SERIES

DO COWS HAVE KITTENS?
A Question and Answer Book
about Animal Babies

DO GOLDFISH FLY?
A Question and Answer Book
about Animal Movements

DO MONKEYS EAT MARSHMALLOWS?
A Question and Answer Book
about Animal Diets

DO WHALES HAVE WHISKERS?
A Question and Answer Book
about Animal Body Parts

INDEX